EXPLORING • SPACE

Rockets

**David Baker
and Heather Kissock**

WEIGL PUBLISHERS INC.

Published by Weigl Publishers Inc.
350 5th Avenue, Suite 3304, PMB 6G
New York, NY 10118-0069

Website: www.weigl.com
Copyright ©2009 WEIGL PUBLISHERS INC.

All of the Internet URLs given in the book were valid at the time of publication. However, due
to the dynamic nature of the Internet, some addresses may have changed, or sites may have
ceased to exist since publication. While the author and publisher regret any inconvenience this
may cause readers, no responsibility for any such changes can be accepted by either the
author or the publisher.

Library of Congress Cataloging-in-Publication Data available upon request.
Fax 1-866-44-WEIGL for the attention of the Publishing Records department.

ISBN 978-1-59036-771-1 (hard cover)
ISBN 978-1-59036-772-8 (soft cover)

Printed in the United States of America
1 2 3 4 5 6 7 8 9 0 12 11 10 09 08

Weigl would like to acknowledge Getty Images and NASA as its primary photo suppliers
for this title.

Every reasonable effort has been made to trace ownership and to obtain permission
to reprint copyright material. The publishers would be pleased to have any errors
or omissions brought to their attention so that they may be corrected in
subsequent printings.

EDITOR: Heather Kissock
DESIGN: Terry Paulhus
LAYOUT: Kathryn Livingstone

Rockets

CONTENTS

What is a Rocket?

A rocket is a powerful means of launching things over great distances. There are many types of rocket. A firework for parties and celebrations is a type of rocket. It is small and flies within the **atmosphere**. Other types of rocket include those that are designed to work in space.

Most rockets are tube-shaped devices that carry a special type of fuel, as well as oxygen to burn the fuel. Together, fuel and oxygen are called the **propellants**. They create the **thrust** to propel the rocket. When the fuel is ignited, gases are released. The force of these gases pushing in one direction causes the tube to move through the air in the opposite direction.

A rocket is the only device that can travel into space. This is because it is does not need air and does not rely on an external force for its power. Everything it needs to power itself is contained within the rocket.

In the past, rockets put both people and equipment in space. With the creation of the space shuttle, rockets are used mainly to transport equipment.

Fireworks are launched into the sky to celebrate important dates in history, such as Independence Day.

BRAIN BOOSTER

The idea of using thrust to move an object forward has been around for centuries. Writings from ancient Rome show that a Greek man by the name of Archytas built a wooden pigeon that used steam to fly. A burst of steam provided the thrust needed to move the pigeon.

About 300 years after Archytas built his pigeon, Hero of Alexandria invented a rocket-like device called an aeolipile. It also used steam to move objects.

Rocket Parts

Rockets come in a range of sizes and have many uses. Rockets that are sent into space, however, have four main parts. These parts are called systems. Each system has its own role in the operation of the rocket.

STRUCTURE

The structure system consists of the rocket's frame. It is made of strong, lightweight materials, such as aluminum. Some rockets have fins attached at the bottom. These help to keep the rocket steady as it soars through the air.

PAYLOAD

The payload system consists of the cargo the rocket is carrying into space. This can include **satellites** and humans.

GUIDANCE

The guidance system is made up of the computers and other technologies that allow the rocket to stay on course so that it arrives at its planned destination.

PROPULSION

The propulsion system is what pushes the rocket into the air and beyond. It is made up of fuel, oxygen, and the machinery needed to operate the motors.

Basics of Thrust

In 1686, Sir Isaac Newton, a British scientist, introduced his laws of motion. One of these laws explained how every action has an equal and opposite reaction. Rockets are an example of this law. A rocket engine produces the action of exhaust gases flowing out the back of the engine. In reaction, a thrusting force is produced in the opposite direction. This propels the rocket into space.

REACTION

ACTION

Solid and Liquid Fueled Rockets

There are two types of rocket propellant. One is solid propellant, and the other is liquid propellant. Solid propellant can take many forms. Some contain tiny grains of a powder that, when ignited, will burn fast with a bright flame. Fireworks are an example of this type of rocket. Another form of solid propellant is like a **resin**. Both types contain a combination of fuel and oxygen. Oxygen and fuel packed together make an **oxidizer**.

Some big solid propellant rockets are built from a series of hollow **cylindrical** sections, one placed on top of the other. There is a rubbery fuel inside the hollow of each cylinder. When ignited, the cylinders burn from the inside out, toward the wall of the cylinder. This produces thrust that escapes out the bottom. NASA uses this kind of solid propellant rocket to launch shuttles into space.

The space shuttle uses both solid and liquid fueled rockets to launch into space.

In a liquid-propellant rocket, fuel is carried in one tank, and a substance that helps the fuel burn, such as oxygen, is carried in another. Both combine inside the engine to produce exhaust that acts as a propellant.

Liquid-propellant rockets are most efficient and are best for space launches. This is because they produce more energy for the same weight of propellant than solid propellant rockets. This helps push them far into space without exhausting the fuel supply. Solid propellant rockets are best for use as **missiles** because they fire faster than liquid-propellant rockets and can gain speed more quickly during liftoff. In times of war, they can get to their target quickly.

Military missiles are used in all divisons of the armed forces. They can be launched at sea, on ground, and from the air.

THINK ABOUT IT
Look around you to see how other machines are powered. Do you think any of these power sources could be used for rockets? How?

Rocket History

The first rockets were used in China more than 800 years ago. Fueled by gunpowder, they were first used as fireworks at parties and gatherings. Later, the Chinese adapted them for use in warfare.

In later centuries, Europeans developed the rocket further as a weapon of war. One rocket was called the Congreve. It used a 16-foot (5-meter) guide stick as a **stabilizer**. This helped the rocket travel distances up to 9,000 feet (2,743 m).

In 1926, American Robert Goddard was the first person to build a liquid-propellant rocket. It had long been known that liquid-propellant rockets would produce more energy than a solid propellant rocket, but no one had been able to build one. Goddard studied the problems associated with getting a liquid rocket to fly and successfully launched the first liquid-fueled rocket.

During World War II, German engineer Wernher von Braun created a rocket missile called the V-2. It traveled so fast and far that it became a main weapon for the Germans throughout the war.

Following the war, von Braun moved to the United States to make rockets for them. There, he developed the Redstone, the first missile built in America to achieve a range of more than 200 miles (322 kilometers). In 1960, von Braun joined NASA, where he worked on making rockets for space travel.

The first Redstone missile was launched on August 20, 1953.

Wernher
von Braun

Wernher von Braun was born in Wirzitz, Germany, on March 12, 1912. After reading science fiction books by Jules Verne and H.G. Wells, he developed an interest in space travel. In school, he worked on mastering mathematics so that he could learn the science behind rocketry. When he finished high school, von Braun was accepted into the Berlin Institute of Technology to study engineering.

Upon graduation in 1932, von Braun went to work for the German army. His job was to create rockets for the military. While working on these projects, he continued his studies and, in 1934, received a **doctorate** in aerospace engineering from the University of Berlin.

von Braun continued his work with the German army in the years leading up to World War II. In 1937, he was sent to a secret site on the Baltic Coast to develop missiles for the war. It was here that the V-2 missile was developed.

Following his move to the United States, von Braun continued designing military rockets. However, when NASA was created in 1960, he became the agency's first director, and his focus turned to developing rockets that would go into space. von Braun had many successes with NASA and played a key role in their rocket program until his retirement in 1972. In 1977, he died of cancer at the age of 65.

Launching Satellites

In the 1950s, small rockets were being sent into space for research purposes. Some were launched with cameras that could look back at Earth. Others carried scientific tools that took measurements and recorded data related to Earth's atmosphere before falling back to Earth. These rockets were called "sounding rockets" because they helped scientists "sound out," or explore, the upper edges of Earth's atmosphere, also known as near-Earth space.

Development and use of sounding rockets gave scientists an interest in putting satellites in **orbit**. This would give the tools the rockets carried a permanent platform in space. The first country to achieve this goal was Russia, when, on October 4, 1957, it launched the first successful satellite, *Sputnik I*. A few months later, the United States sent their first satellite, *Explorer I*, into space.

A Jupiter-C rocket called Juno I lifted *Explorer I* into space. Jupiter-C rockets were a later version of the Redstone missile.

Rockets are still used to launch satellites and other equipment into space. These rockets are often called launch vehicles. Since the first Russian satellite launched in 1957, countries around the world have been using launch vehicles to send satellites into space.

The rocket engines used for launching satellites are very powerful. The rocket acts as a motor to push the satellite upward. The entire structure of the rocket, including the motor and the fuel tanks, is called an **Expendable** Launch Vehicle, or ELV. The main body of the rocket separates from the satellite after it reaches orbit. When the launch vehicle and satellite reach orbit, the motor shuts down, and the satellite is released into space.

In 2005, a Russian Soyuz rocket was launched with a navigation satellite called *Galileo* onboard.

GET CONNECTED

To find out more about expendable launch vehicles, go to www.britannica.com/eb/article-9047343/launch-vehicle.

Rockets
from Russia

Like many other countries, Russia developed solid and liquid propellant rockets during World War II. After the war, Russia kept making rockets and missiles that could be used in the event of another war. One of the most important rockets to be made after the war was the R-7 intercontinental **ballistic missile** (ICBM). At first, it was designed to carry warheads as far as 5,468 miles (8,800 km). However, the R-7 became better known as a satellite launcher. In fact, Russia used the R-7 to launch *Sputnik I* and other satellites into space. Over time, changes have been made to the rocket so that it has greater lifting power. Now called Soyuz, the rocket is still used to launch satellites and send astronauts from around the world to the International Space Station, a research center located in space.

Proton rockets began launching in 1965 and are still being used today to launch satellites for the Russian government, as well as international companies.

Russia has built other rockets as well. The biggest Russian rocket is called Proton. It was designed in the early 1960s as a missile but was never used as one. Instead, it was made into an Expendable Launch Vehicle for satellites and spacecraft. Proton made its first flight in 1965. With a thrust of 1,050 tons (953 tonnes), it can put satellites weighing more than 20 tons (18.5 t) in orbit.

Soyuz rockets are put together horizontally. They are placed in a vertical position when they reach the launch pad.

A still bigger rocket, called N1, also was built in the 1960s. It was meant to send Russian astronauts to the Moon. Only a few were built and tested, but they all failed shortly after launch. Production of the N1 stopped. Later, the ideas behind the N1 were used to make a rocket called Energia. Energia which was meant to launch Russia's version of the space shuttle, *Buran*, into space. However, both the rocket and the space shuttle stopped production when the **Soviet Union** disbanded in 1991.

BRAIN BOOSTER

In 1957, a second *Sputnik* satellite was sent into space using an R-7 rocket. *Sputnik 2* carried a dog named Laika onboard, making her the first Earthling to be sent into space.

Rockets from the R-7 family were used to build the International Space Station. They launched supply ships and lifeboats for the station's crew.

The Soyuz rocket is the only launch vehicle in Russia that carries people into space.

The United States
Rocket Program

While Russia was developing its rockets, the United States also was inventing new rocket technology, including multi-stage rockets. In the past, rockets used a single engine to travel. When the rocket ran out of fuel, it stopped gaining speed. This limited the distance the rocket could travel. The United States decided to make rockets that had two stages, each with its own fuel. The bottom part of the rocket carried the greatest amount of fuel and pushed the rocket the farthest distance. When its fuel ran out, the bottom dropped away, and the top used its own fuel to keep moving forward.

Over time, more stages were used to make rockets that could reach farther distances. In 1958, a four-stage rocket was used to launch the first U.S. satellite, *Explorer I*, into space.

The United States government decided to create an organization that would develop technology for space exploration. In 1958, President Eisenhower announced the creation of the National Aeronatics and Space Administration, or NASA. This was followed by the construction of the Kennedy Space Center at Cape Canaveral, Florida.

Since its creation, NASA has been responsible for some of the greatest moments in space travel.

Space
Race

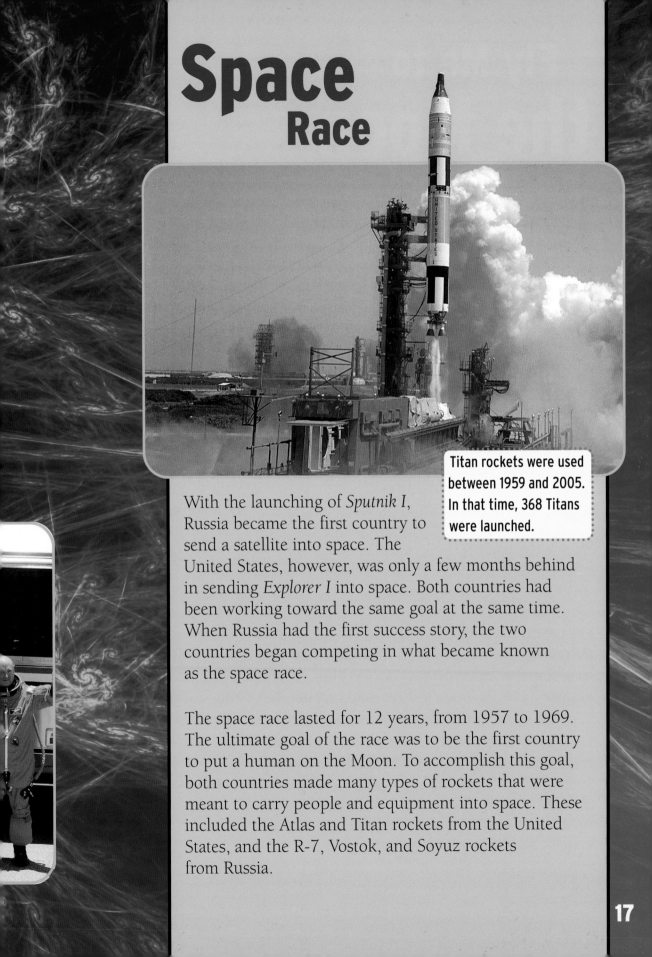

Titan rockets were used between 1959 and 2005. In that time, 368 Titans were launched.

With the launching of *Sputnik I*, Russia became the first country to send a satellite into space. The United States, however, was only a few months behind in sending *Explorer I* into space. Both countries had been working toward the same goal at the same time. When Russia had the first success story, the two countries began competing in what became known as the space race.

The space race lasted for 12 years, from 1957 to 1969. The ultimate goal of the race was to be the first country to put a human on the Moon. To accomplish this goal, both countries made many types of rockets that were meant to carry people and equipment into space. These included the Atlas and Titan rockets from the United States, and the R-7, Vostok, and Soyuz rockets from Russia.

Fly Me to the Moon

The VAB is more than 400 feet (122 m) tall—so big it can contain all the pyramids of Egypt clustered together.

In 1961, President John F. Kennedy gave NASA a **mandate** to put two people on the Moon before 1970. This launched NASA's Apollo space program. The main goal of this program was to create a spacecraft that could carry three people into space, land on the Moon, and then bring the people back to Earth.

Before sending people to the Moon, NASA sent robots to find out as much as possible about the surface. Atlas missiles were used to send robot explorers to the surface of the Moon. The Atlas was the most powerful rocket of its time, producing a thrust of about 175 tons (159 t).

On Earth, scientists were constructing a plan to land people on the Moon. Part of this plan included the building of a powerful rocket. Wernher von Braun designed the Saturn V, a three-stage rocket, to do the job.

Each of the rocket stages was built at different places across the United States and were brought to the Kennedy Space Center for assembly. To stack together the stages of the Saturn V and prepare it for launch, NASA built a giant shed at the northern end of Cape Canaveral called the Vehicle Assembly Building, or VAB.

The stages of the Saturn V were put together on a **mobile launch platform**. Upon completion, the Saturn V was 363 feet (111 m) tall—60 feet (18 m) taller than the Statue of Liberty on its pedestal. It weighed 3,000 tons (2,722 t) fully fuelled.

The *Apollo* spacecraft was lifted by crane from the floor of the VAB and placed on top of Saturn V's third stage. A specially designed vehicle was driven under the mobile launch platform. The vehicle lifted the mobile platform, complete with Saturn V rocket, and slowly drove the Saturn V to the launch pad, 3 miles (4.8 km) away. When the vehicle arrived at the pad, it lowered Saturn V onto it. The crawler then backed out from under the mobile platform, and the rocket was ready for launch. At liftoff, Saturn V produced a thrust of more than 3,750 tons (3,402 t). This was enough to send the *Apollo* spacecraft to the Moon, where it landed on July 20, 1969. With this success, the United States became the winner of the space race.

The Saturn V was used as part of the Apollo space program. When the Apollo program was cancelled, the Saturn V was retired from active use.

THINK ABOUT IT

There are many details to consider when designing a rocket that will take people into space. How big should the rocket be? How many stages should it be to get it into space? Should the astronauts travel inside the rocket or in an attached vehicle? What are the advantages and disadvantages of the option you have selected?

In Orbit

During the 1970s, NASA developed the space shuttle to replace all expendable launch vehicles. The shuttle would launch satellites and spacecraft and return satellites to Earth for repair. Flights began in 1981, but the shuttle became too expensive to use for launching satellites. For this reason, ELVs continue to be used today. ELVs act as delivery trucks, carrying satellites and spacecraft to different orbits.

The shuttle is now used as a reusable transport ship for carrying people and cargo to and from the International Space Station. The shuttle uses both solid and liquid propellant motors.

The Saturn V launch sites were modified to allow the shuttle to be launched from the same pads built for the Apollo program.

Its tail holds three powerful liquid propellant engines that, together, provide about 600 tons (544 t) of thrust at launch. On either side of the shuttle are two solid rocket boosters, or SRBs, with a combined thrust of about 3,000 tons (2,722 t). The SRBs provide the thrust to lift the shuttle off the pad. These SRBs fire for only two minutes before they separate from the shuttle. The shuttle then relies on its liquid-propellant rockets to push it into space. In the meantime, three giant parachutes gently lower the SRBs into the Atlantic Ocean, where they are recovered for use on future space shuttle launches.

Orion

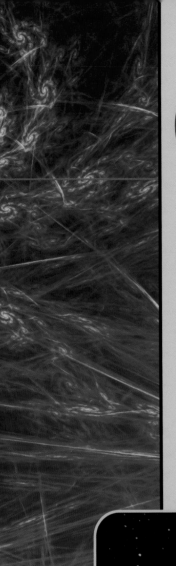

The shuttle will continue to take people into space until about 2010, when it will be replaced by another spacecraft called *Orion*. The launch vehicle for *Orion* will be a single, lengthened version of the shuttle's solid rocket booster, called Ares I.

Orion and Ares I will build on technology used to create the shuttle and other spacecraft. The plan is to create a more advanced spacecraft that has multiple uses. NASA is planning a return to space exploration and intends to send humans back to the Moon by 2020. This is to be followed by landings on Mars and other places within the solar system. *Orion* and Ares I are the spacecraft targeted for these missions.

Artists have created pictures that show what *Orion* will look like when completed.

Making
the Grade

Working with rockets requires people to have very specific skills and education. Rocket specialists must have a good grasp of science principles, along with strong technical skills. They must be detail-oriented people who strive to improve current technologies. With these traits and qualifications, there are many career paths that can be taken.

ASTRONAUTICAL ENGINEER

Astronautical engineers design, develop, and test spacecraft and rockets. They often specialize in very specific areas, such as structural design and navigation or communication systems. It is their job to create equipment and vehicles that can survive the journey from Earth to space and back again. They need to have expert knowledge on the conditions the equipment will experience so that the correct materials and technology are used to create it. They are involved in the construction process from design to finished product.

ASTRONAUT QUALIFICATIONS

CITIZENSHIP

Pilots and mission specialists must be U.S. citizens. Payload specialists can be from other countries.

EDUCATION

Astronauts must have a minimum bachelor's degree in engineering, biology, physics, or mathematics. Most astronauts have a doctorate.

ROCKET TECHNICIAN

Rocket technicians are involved in putting rockets together. Their work is very detailed and must be done properly so that the rocket meets all safety standards. They must inspect all of the parts that will be assembled to make sure that there are no flaws that could cause problems during launch. When the safety of the rocket is confirmed, the technicians are responsible for transporting it safely to the launch pad. They then assist in the final launch preparations so that the launch runs smoothly.

PILOT ASTRONAUT

A pilot astronaut guides spacecraft into space and brings it back to Earth. These astronauts are responsible for the safety of the vehicle, the equipment inside, and the crew. Pilot astronauts must have strong knowledge about the scientific processes that propel their spacecraft into space and be able to apply this knowledge to the launch, flight, and landing of the spacecraft. Many pilot astronauts have engineering degrees for this reason.

EXPERIENCE

Astronauts must have at least three years of experience in a science-related field. Pilots must have jet experience with more than 1,000 hours of in-command flight time.

HEALTH

All astronauts must pass a NASA physical, with specific vision and blood pressure requirements.

HEIGHT

Pilots must be 64 to 76 inches (162.5 to 193 cm) tall. Mission or payload specialists must be 58.5 to 76 inches (148.5 to 193 cm) tall.

A Day
in Space

When astronauts go into space, they work as part of a NASA team. A day in space usually has a set schedule. The crew will awake to either the sound of an alarm clock, or the blast of a song over the speaker system. For breakfast, the astronauts eat a meal that they chose before launch. After eating, it is time for the astronauts to brush their teeth and get ready for work.

A list, known as the flight plan, tells the crew what they are to work on each day. Sometimes, there is need for a spacewalk. Other times, the crew carries out housekeeping duties, such as trash collection and cleaning. Breaks, such as lunch and dinner, are also scheduled throughout the day. Keeping fit in such a confined space is very important as well, so blocks of time are put aside for the astronauts to set up and use exercise equipment. At the end of the workday, the astronauts may read a book or listen to music.

Teamwork is an essential part of life in space. Astronauts live in a confined space for days. They must all work together to make the trip comfortable for everyone on board.

The Daily Schedule

8:30 to 10:00 a.m.: Post-sleep (Morning station inspection, breakfast, morning **hygiene**)

10:00 to 10:30 a.m.: Planning and coordination (Daily planning conference and status report)

10:30 a.m. to 1:00 p.m.: Exercise (Set-up exercise equipment, exercise, and put equipment away)

1:00 to 2:00 p.m.: Lunch, personal hygiene

2:00 to 3:30 p.m.: Daily systems operations (Work preparation, report writing, emails, to-do list review, trash collection)

3:30 to 10:00 p.m.: Work (Work set-up and maintenance, performing experiments and payload operations, checking positioning and operating systems)

10:00 p.m. to 12:00 a.m.: Pre-sleep (food preparation, evening meal, and hygiene)

12:00 to 8:30 a.m.: Sleep

The work that astronauts do on the shuttle is serious, but there is always time to enjoy the experience of being in space.

Rocketing
the World

Today, many countries and organizations around the world have space programs. The Ariane, a very powerful ELV, was one of the first projects from the **European Space Agency**. Europeans began working on the Ariane series of ELVs in the early 1970s, when NASA first started making the shuttle. Ariane was designed to put communication satellites in space so that they could relay their television, telephone, and radio signals around the planet. First launched in 1979, the original Ariane I has been developed into the powerful Ariane V that is in use today. To date, Ariane has launched almost half of the world's commercial satellites.

All Ariane V launches occur in Kourou, French Guiana, near the equator. Rockets launched close to the equator get an extra boost from Earth's rotation. They do not use as much fuel as a result.

China has already launched people into space, only the third country after Russia and the United States to do so. The first Chinese astronaut was launched into space on October 15, 2003. That was followed by a two-man flight two years later that lasted almost five days. Since the 1980s, Chinese launch vehicles have been transporting satellites supplied by other countries, including the United States and Europe. It does so at less cost than rockets operated by these places.

Some people see the greatest advantage of space programs as the co-operation they encourage between different people around the world. Rockets and satellite launchers have helped make that possible.

Like NASA, China's space program has its own version of a vehicle assembly building.

Test Your
Knowledge

1 What is the name of the force that propels rockets into the air?

Thrust

2 What are two types of rocket propellant?

Liquid and solid

3 What was the name of the German scientist who developed rockets for NASA?

Wernher von Braun

4 What were the first rockets sent into space called?

Sounding rockets

5 What was name of the first satellite to reach space?

Sputnik 1

6 What do the letters ELV stand for?

Expendable Launch Vehicle

7 When was NASA created?

July 29, 1958

8 What was the name of the rocket NASA used to send people to the Moon?

Saturn V

10 What organization developed the Ariane ELV?

European Space Agency

9 Where does NASA launch its space vehicles from?

Kennedy Space Center

Further
Resources

How can I find out more about rockets?

Most libraries have computers that connect to a database for researching information. If you input a key word, you will be provided with a list of books in the library that contain information on that topic. Non-fiction books are arranged numerically, using their call number. Fiction books are organized alphabetically by the author's last name.

Websites

To learn more about the history of rockets, visit **http://history.msfc.nasa.gov/rocketry**.

For information about rockets used for space travel and research, go to **www.aerospaceguide.net/spacerocket/index.html**.

The science behind rocketry can be explored at **www.howstuffworks.com/rocket1.htm**.

Glossary

atmosphere: the layer of gases that surrounds Earth

ballistic missile: a type of rocket that has no wings and stays on course when its power source is used up

cylindrical: shaped like a tube

doctorate: an advanced university degree

European Space Agency: an organization formed to develop Europe's space capabilities

expendable: able to be used up and discarded

hygiene: the process of keeping clean

mandate: an official command

missiles: rocket-propelled weapons

mobile launch platform: a structure that is used to move the space shuttle from the assembly building to the launch pad

orbit: the path a satellite or other spacecraft travels around a planet or other space object

oxidizer: something that undergoes a chemical reaction with oxygen

propellants: fuels for a liquid rocket

resin: a waxlike substance

satellites: spacecraft that move in orbit around Earth, the Moon, or other bodies in space and send signals to Earth

Soviet Union: a former communist country in eastern Europe and northern Asia that was established in 1922 and officially dissolved in 1991

stabilizer: a device that keeps an object balanced and steady

thrust: the force that occurs when an object is pushed

Index